ANCIENT MYTHOLOGY
NORSE MYTHS AND LEGENDS

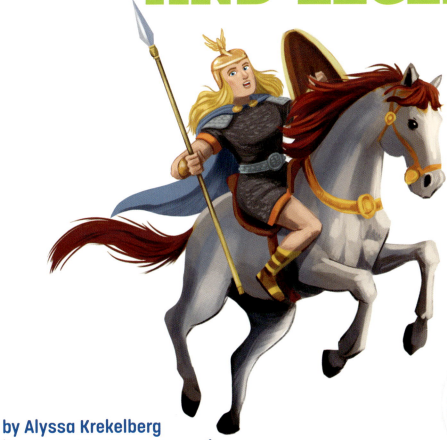

by Alyssa Krekelberg
illustrated by Cesar Samaniego

GRASSHOPPER

Tools for Parents & Teachers

Grasshopper Books enhance imagination and introduce the earliest readers to fun storylines and illustrations. The easy-to-read text supports early reading experiences with repetitive sentence patterns and sight words.

Before Reading

- Discuss the cover illustration. What do readers see?

- Look at the glossary together. Discuss the words.

During Reading

- "Walk" through the book with the reader. Discuss new or unfamiliar words. Sound them out together.

- Look at the illustrations. When and where does the story take place? What is happening in the story?

After Reading

- Prompt the child to think more. Ask: What is your favorite Norse myth? Why?

Grasshopper Books are published by Jump!
3500 American Blvd W, Suite 150
Bloomington, MN 55431
www.jumplibrary.com

Copyright © 2026 Jump! International copyright reserved in all countries. No part of this book may be reproduced in any form without written permission from the publisher.

Jump! is a division of FlutterBee Education Group.

Library of Congress Cataloging-in-Publication Data

Names: Krekelberg, Alyssa, author.
Samaniego, César, 1975- illustrator.
Title: Norse myths and legends / by Alyssa Krekelberg; illustrated by Cesar Samaniego.
Description: Minneapolis, MN: Jump!, Inc., 2026.
Series: Ancient mythology | Includes index.
Audience: Ages 7-10
Identifiers: LCCN 2024044360 (print)
LCCN 2024044361 (ebook)
ISBN 9798892137591 (hardcover)
ISBN 9798892137607 (paperback)
ISBN 9798892137614 (ebook)
Subjects: LCSH: Mythology, Norse–Juvenile literature.
Classification: LCC BL860 .K74 2026 (print)
LCC BL860 (ebook)
DDC 398.20948–dc23/eng/20241206
LC record available at https://lccn.loc.gov/2024044360
LC ebook record available at https://lccn.loc.gov/2024044361

Editor: Katie Chanez
Direction and Layout: Anna Peterson
Illustrator: Cesar Samaniego
Content Consultant: Scott A. Mellor, PhD; Teaching Professor; Department of German, Nordic, and Slavic; University of Wisconsin-Madison

Printed in the United States of America at Corporate Graphics in North Mankato, Minnesota.

Table of Contents

Gods and Giants 4
Norse Gods and Goddesses 22
To Learn More 23
Glossary 24
Index 24

Gods and Giants

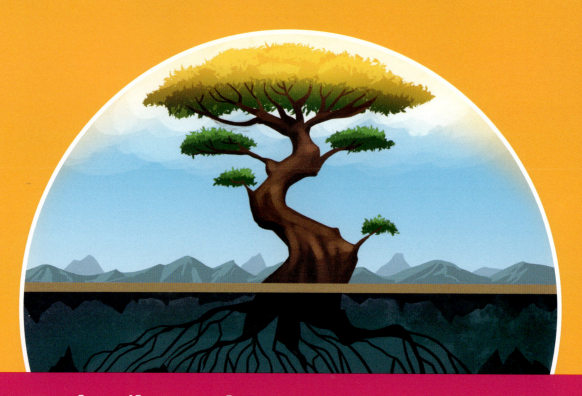

Yggdrasil was a large tree. Its top branches touched the Norse heavens. Its roots reached the **underworld**. It supported the universe. It was the tree of knowledge.

Odin was king of the Norse gods. He had two ravens that flew around the world and told him what they saw. Odin hung on Yggdrasil's branch for nine nights to gain more knowledge. He became the most powerful god!

Norsemen were people who lived long ago in Norway, Sweden, and Denmark. They believed gods and goddesses could change the world. They believed Odin helped **Vikings** in battle. He rode his eight-legged horse. Stories about the Norse gods are known as Norse **mythology**.

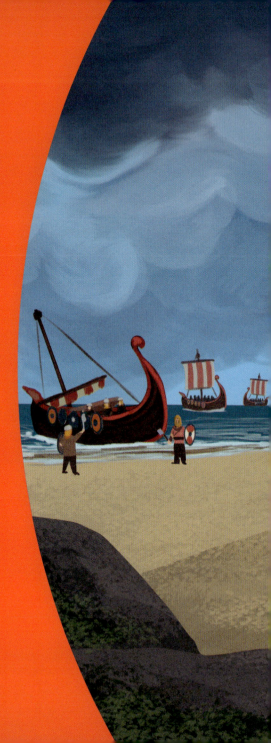

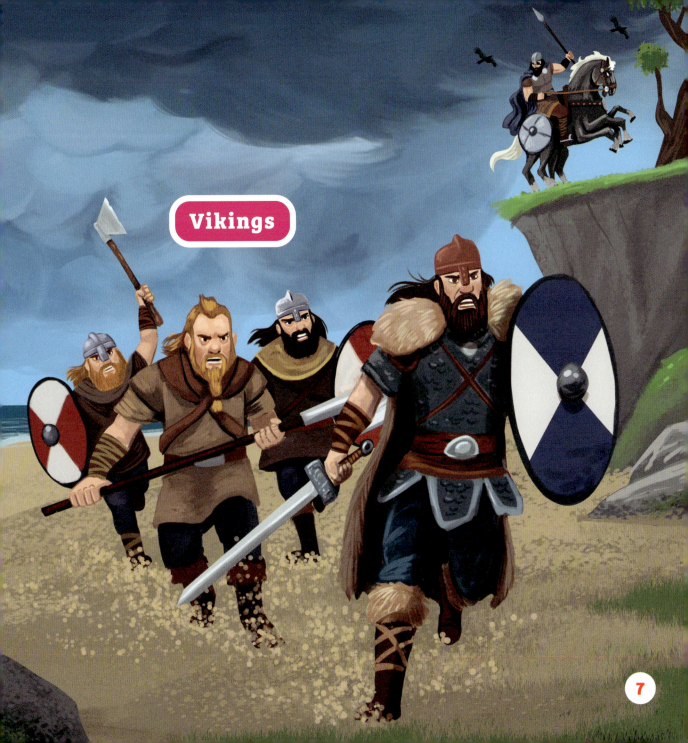

Odin sent Valkyries to battlefields. These women found brave fallen **warriors**. They brought them to Valhalla.

Valhalla was a grand hall. Odin ruled it. Warriors healed here. They **trained**. A mighty battle called Ragnarök was coming. Odin needed the warriors to fight with him.

The gods lived in Asgard. They wanted a large wall to protect them from enemies. A giant said he could build a wall in one winter. In return, he wanted the Sun and Moon. He also wanted to marry Freya, the goddess of love.

The gods did not think it was possible to build a wall so quickly. But the giant used a huge horse to carry heavy rocks. The gods panicked.

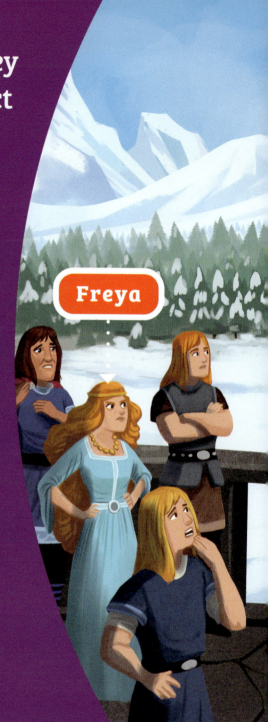

Freya

Loki was the trickster god. He made the giant's horse run away. The giant could not finish his work. He was angry. He attacked the gods.

Thor was the god of thunder. He threw his magic hammer at the giant. Asgard was safe!

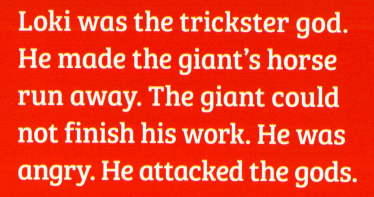

A different giant once tested Thor's strength. First, Thor had to drink all the liquid in a cup. He took three large gulps. But the cup was still full. He had to lift a large cat, too. But he could only lift one paw.

Last, Thor wrestled an old woman. She beat him! It was all a trick. The liquid was the sea. It could not be drained. The cat was a serpent wrapped around the world. No one could move it. And the woman was old age. No one could beat old age. Even the gods had **limits**.

Idun was the goddess of youth. She had magic apples. They kept the gods young. One day, a giant took Idun and her apples. The gods grew older. They were close to death.

Loki turned into a bird. He flew to the giant's home. He turned Idun into a nut and carried her back to Asgard. Idun gave apples to the gods. She saved them from death.

Frigg was the goddess of marriage and motherhood. She knew people's **fates**. She dreamed her son Balder would die. To stop this, Frigg made all things promise not to hurt him. But she did not ask for mistletoe's promise.

One day, Balder was shot with an arrow made of mistletoe. He died. Not even the gods could escape fate.

The ground trembled. Monsters attacked Asgard. The battle of Ragnarök was here! Many gods and people died.

Two people hid in Yggdrasil's branches. After the battle, they came out. They helped make a new world. Gods gathered in Asgard. Balder came back to life. They shared stories of their past adventures.

Norse Gods and Goddesses

Who are Norse mythology's most important gods and goddesses? Take a look!

Balder
God of light

Freya
Goddess of love. She was the twin sister of Freyr.

Freyr
God of harvest. He was the twin brother of Freya.

Frigg
Goddess of motherhood and marriage. She was Odin's wife and Balder's mother.

Heimdall
Watchman of the gods

Idun
Goddess of youth

Loki
Trickster god

Odin
God of war and wisdom.
King of the gods.

Thor
God of thunder

Tyr
God of war

To Learn More

Finding more information is as easy as 1, 2, 3.

❶ Go to www.factsurfer.com
❷ Enter "**Norsemythsandlegends**" into the search box.
❸ Choose your book to see a list of websites.

Glossary

fates: Destinies, or forces that control events and people's lives.

limits: Points beyond which people cannot go.

mythology: A group of stories from a particular culture or religion.

trained: Taught or practiced a skill over a period of time.

underworld: A place in myths where the dead go.

Vikings: Norsemen who invaded the coasts of Europe and explored the North American coast between 701 and 1100 CE.

warriors: People who fight in a battle or war.

Index

Asgard 10, 12, 16, 20

Balder 18, 20

fates 18

Freya 10

Frigg 18

giant 10, 12, 14, 16

hammer 12

Idun 16

Loki 12, 16

Odin 5, 6, 8, 9

Ragnarök 9, 20

Thor 12, 14, 15

underworld 4

Valhalla 8, 9

Valkyries 8

Vikings 6

warriors 8, 9

Yggdrasil 4, 5, 20